PIANO • VOCAL • CHORDS

2009 GREATEST Pop & Rock Hits

THE BIGGEST HITS ★ THE GREATEST ARTISTS
DELUXE ANNUAL EDITION ★

CONTENTS

Alfred Music Publishing Co., Inc.
16320 Roscoe Blvd., Suite 100
P.O. Box 10003
Van Nuys, CA 91410-0003
alfred.com

ISBN-10: 0-7390-6175-5
ISBN-13: 978-0-7390-6175-6

2009
2009
2009

1, 2, 3, 4

Words and Music by
TOM HIGGENSON

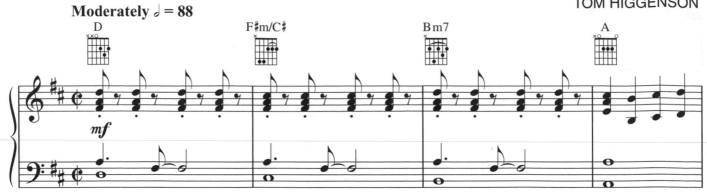

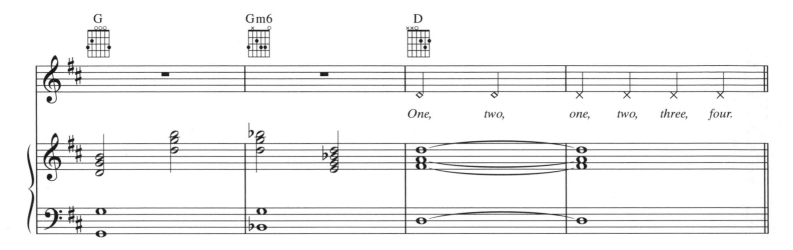

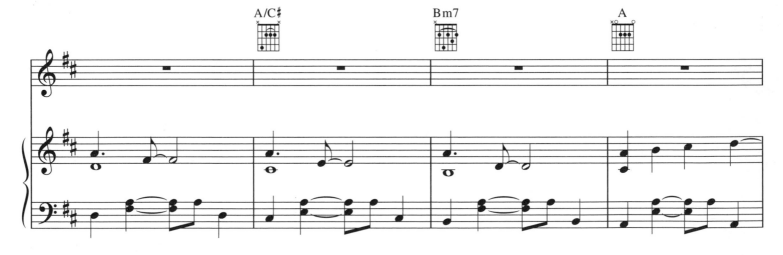

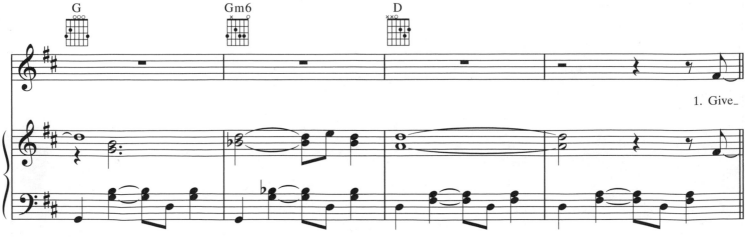

Verse:

me more lov-in' that I've ev-er had,__ make__ it all bet-ter when I'm
me more lov-in' from the ver-y start,__ piece__ me back to-geth-er when I

feel-ing sad,__ tell__ me that I'm spe-cial e-ven when I know__ I'm not.__
fall a-part,__ tell__ me things you nev-er e-ven tell your clos-est friends._

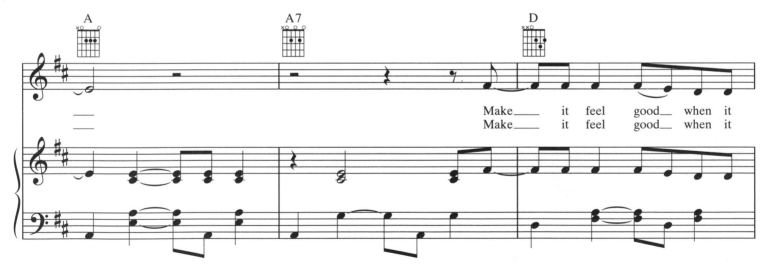

Make__ it feel good__ when it
Make__ it feel good__ when it

hurts so bad,__ bare-ly get mad.} I'm__ so glad__ I found_
hurts so bad,__ best__ that I've had.}

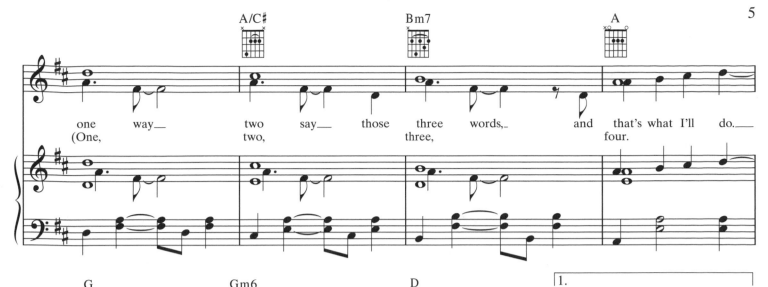

one way___   two   say___ those three words,___   and   that's what I'll   do.___
(One,   two,   three,   four.

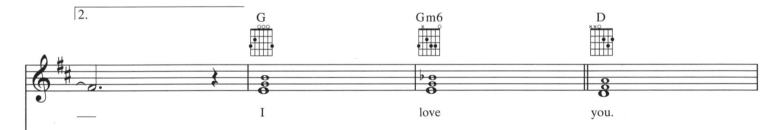

___   I love___ you._____   Give__
            I   love   you.)

___   I   love   you.

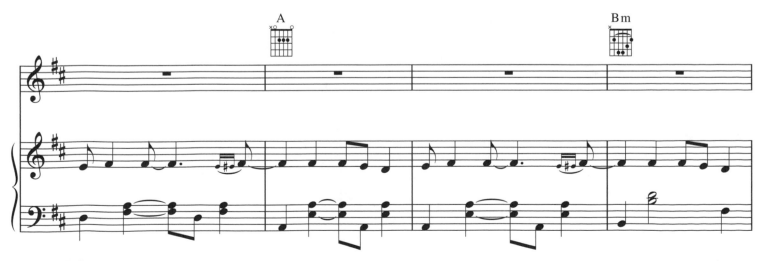

6

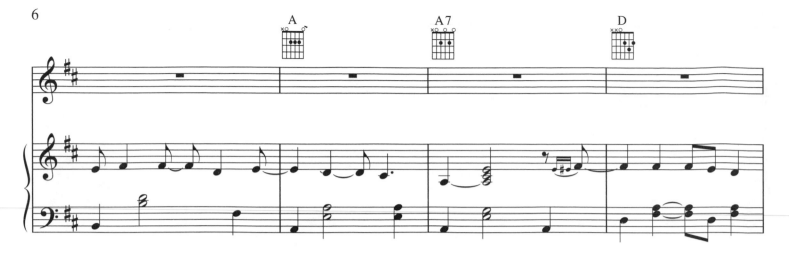

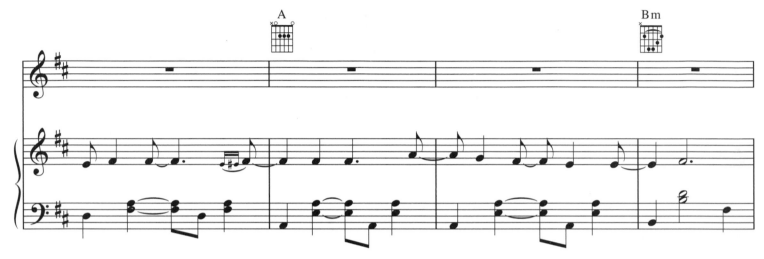

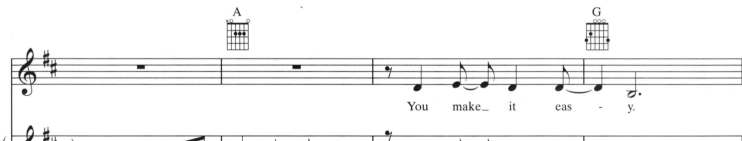

You make_ it eas - y.

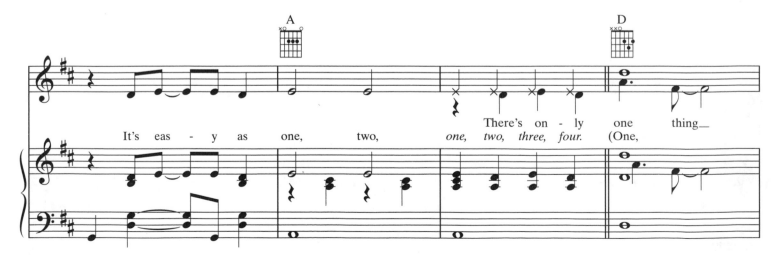

It's eas - y as one, two, *one, two, three, four.* (One, There's on - ly one thing_

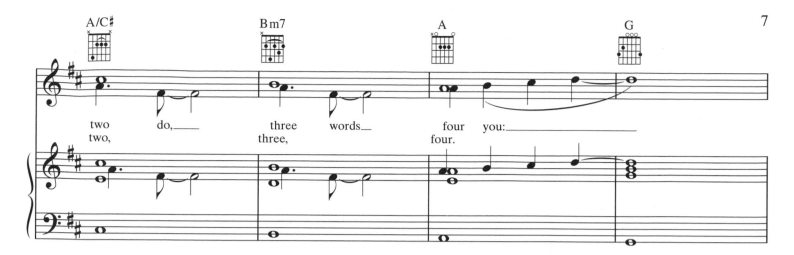

two   do,_____   three   words___   four   you:_____
two,   three,   four.

          I   love_____   you.   There's   on - ly   one   way___
     I   love   you.)   (One,

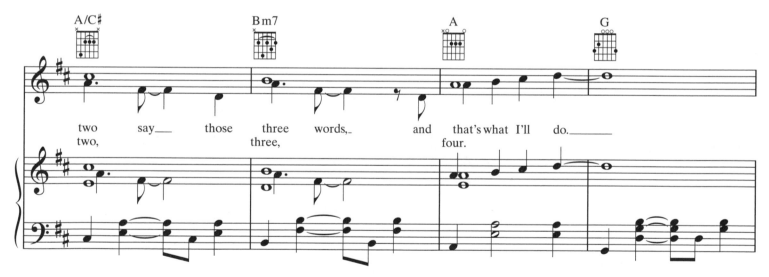

two   say___   those   three   words,_   and   that's what I'll   do._____
two,   three,   four.

          I   love___   you._____
     I   love   you.)

8

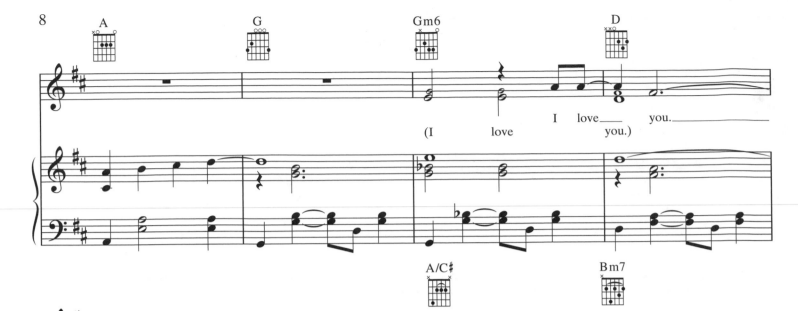

I love___ you.___
(I love I love you.)

___
(One, two, three,

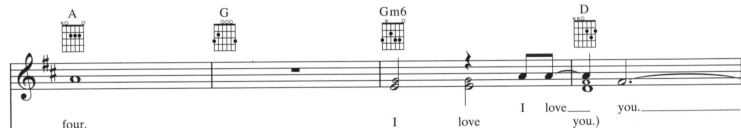

four. I love I love___ you.___

___
(I love you.)
I love___ you.

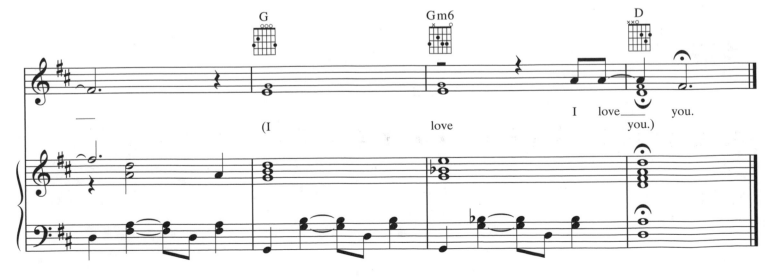

1, 2, 3, 4 - 7 - 7

AT LAST

Lyrics by
MACK GORDON

Music by
HARRY WARREN

10

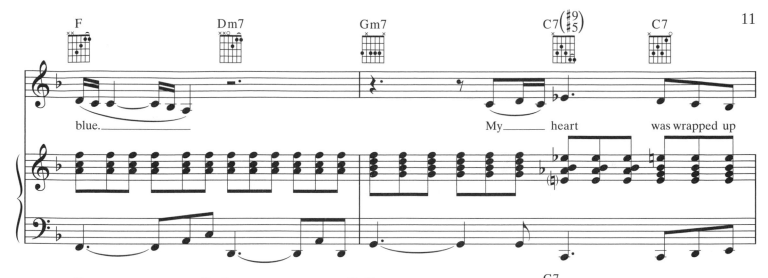

blue._____ My_____ heart was wrapped up

in clo - ver_____ the night I_____ looked at

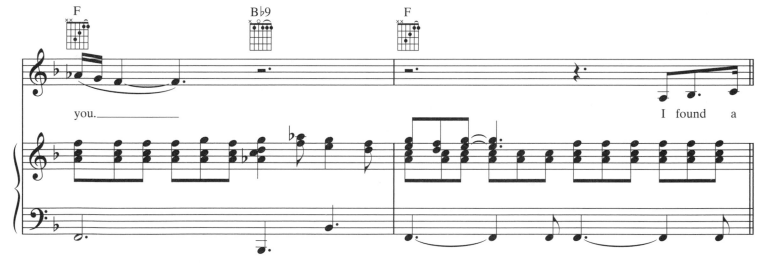

you._____ I found a

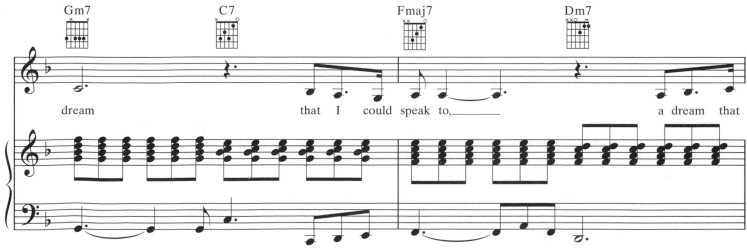

dream that I could speak to,_____ a dream that

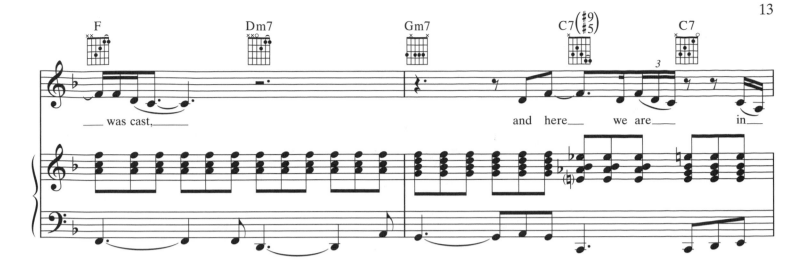

was cast,_____ and here___ we are___ in___

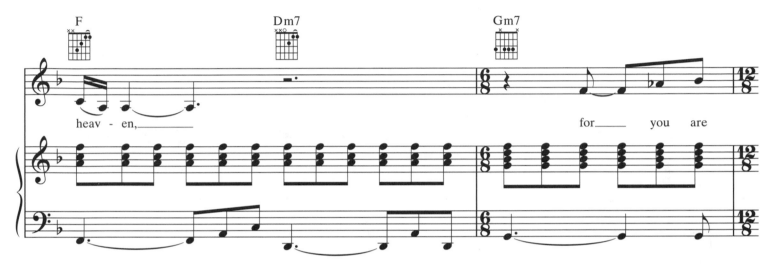

heav - en,_____ for___ you are

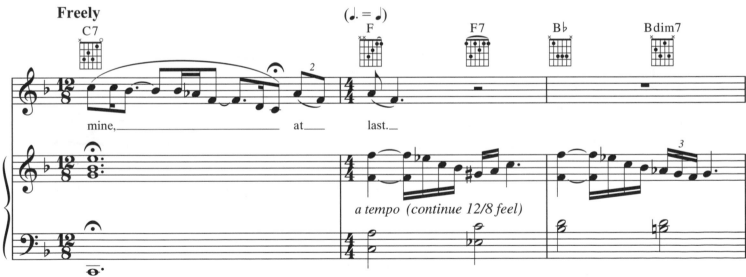

mine,_____ at___ last.___

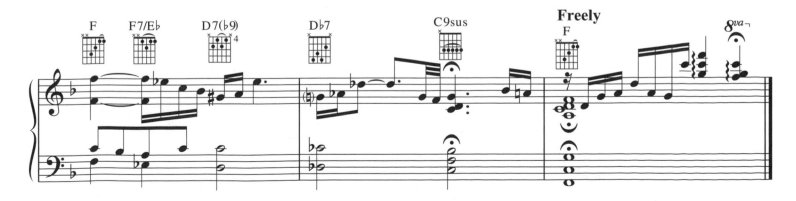

ALL SUMMER LONG

Words and Music by MATTHEW SHAFER, R.J. RITCHIE,
WARREN ZEVON, LEROY MARINELL, WADDY WACHTEL,
ED KING, GARY ROSSINGTON and RONNIE VAN ZANT

18

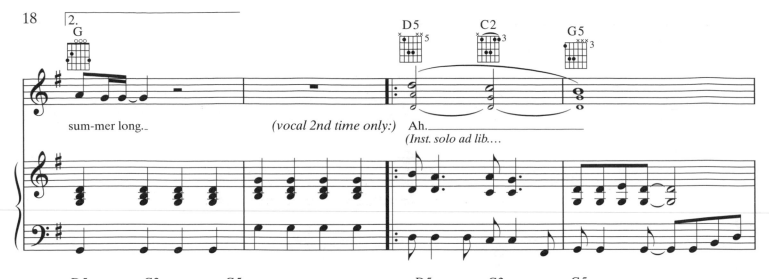

sum-mer long._   *(vocal 2nd time only:)*   Ah._____

(Inst. solo ad lib....

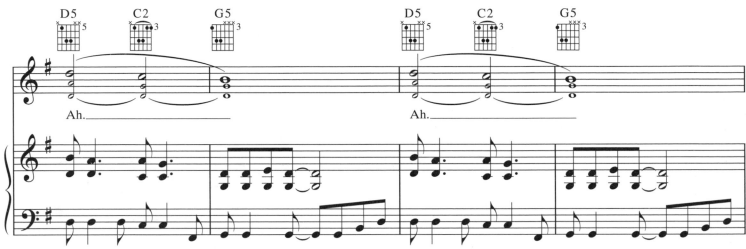

Ah.   Ah.

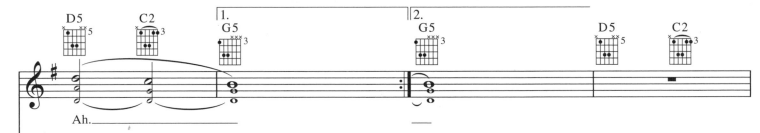

Ah._____

D.S. % al Coda

4. Now,
...end solo)

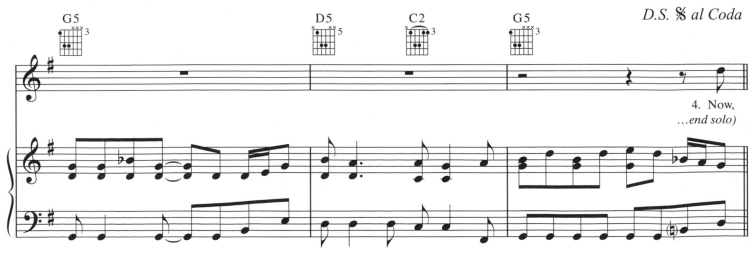

sum-mer long.___ Sing-in' "Sweet_Home Al-a-bam-a"___ all sum-mer long.___

Ah.___

Ah.___

Freely

ANGELS ON THE MOON

Music and Lyrics by
SCOTT JASON with CLAYTON STROOPE

Verse 1:

dream___ that the world will know___ your name?___ So tell___ me your

Angels on the Moon - 8 - 1

24

26

28

Angels on the Moon - 8 - 7

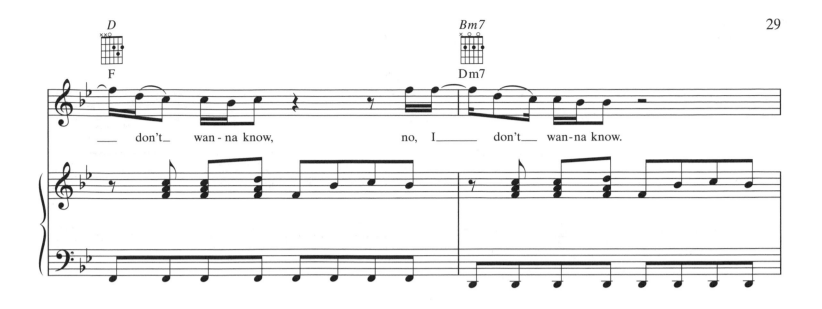

don't_ wan - na know,   no, I____ don't__ wan-na know.

Don't tell me if____ I'm dy -

ing.____   Don't tell me if__ I'm dy - ing.____

BROKEN

Words and Music by
JASON WADE

Slowly ♩ = 69

(with pedal)

1. The

Verse 1:

bro-ken clock__ is a com-fort, it helps me sleep__ to-night.

May-be it can__ stop to-mor-row from steal-ing all__ my__ time.__ And

* Original recording in B, guitars tuned down 1/2 step.

Broken - 8 - 1

32

there is heal - ing. In your name,___

I find mean - ing. So I'm hold - in' on,___

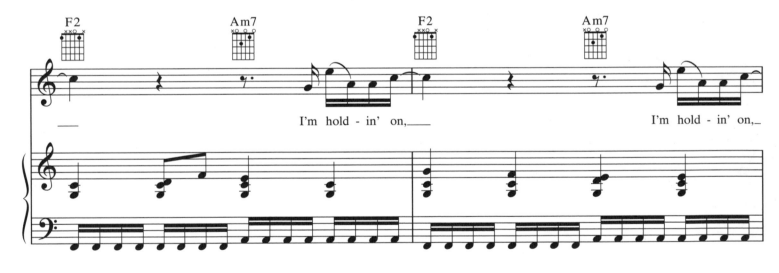

I'm hold - in' on,___ I'm hold - in' on,___

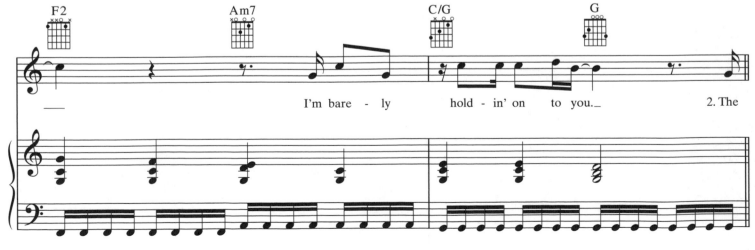

I'm bare - ly hold - in' on to you.___ 2. The

Broken - 8 - 3

Verse 2:

bro-ken locks__ were a warn - ing you got in - side__ my head. I

tried my best__ to be guard - ed,__ I'm an o - pen book__ in-stead. And

I still see__ your re - flec - tion in - side__ of my eyes,__

that are look - ing for pur - pose, they're still look - ing for life.__ I'm fall-ing a - part,__

Broken - 8 - 4

§ *Chorus:*

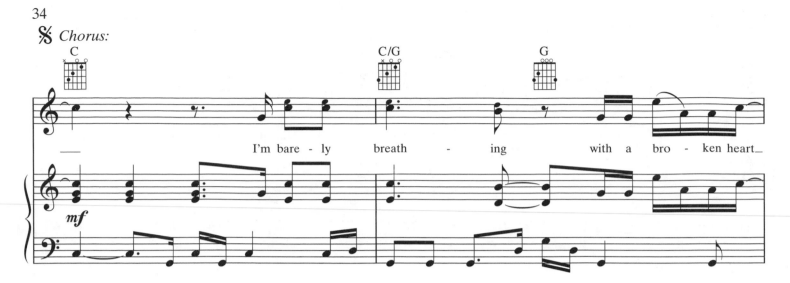

I'm bare - ly breath - ing with a bro - ken heart_

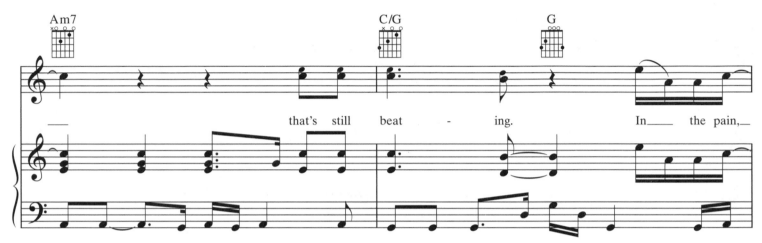

that's still beat - ing. In___ the pain,_

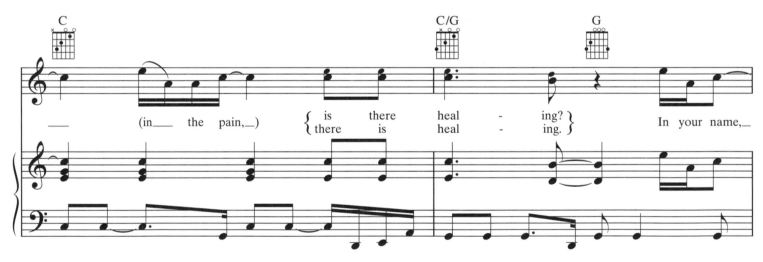

(in___ the pain,_) { is there heal - ing? }
{ there is heal - ing. } In your name,_

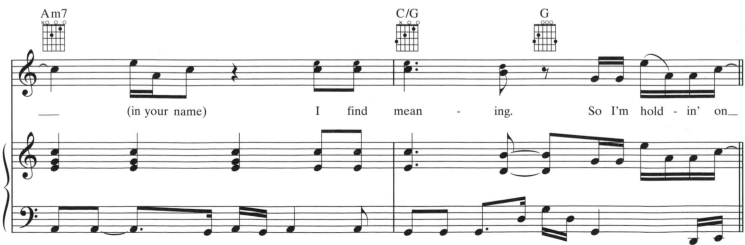

(in your name) I find mean - ing. So I'm hold - in' on_

To Coda

I'm hold - in' on,_____ I'm hold - in' on,__
(I'm_ still hold - in', I'm hold - in' on._____ I'm_ still hold - in',

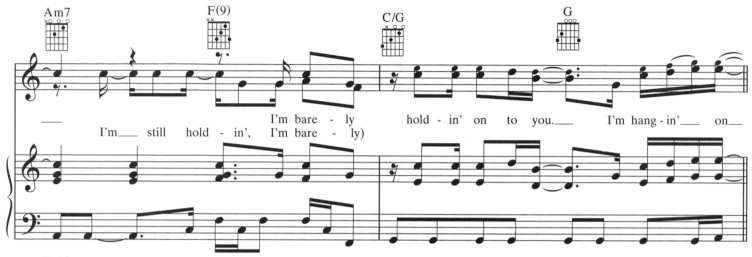

I'm bare - ly hold - in' on to you._ I'm hang - in'_ on_
I'm_ still hold - in', I'm bare - ly)

Bridge:

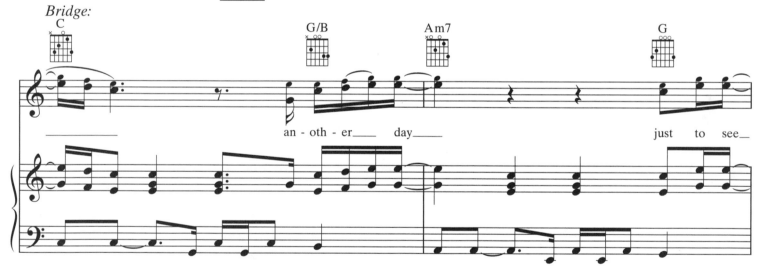

an - oth - er_ day_ just to see_

__ what_ you will throw my way._ And I'm hang - in' on_

Broken - 8 - 6

36

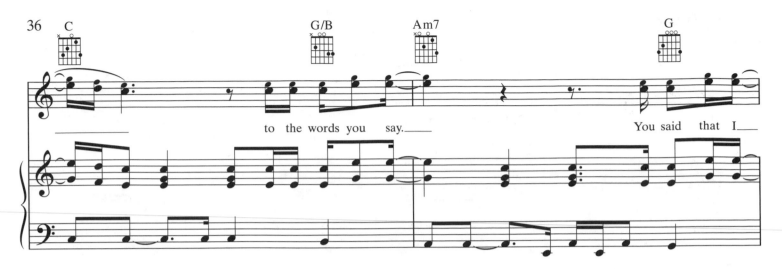

to the words you say.___ You said that I___

___ will___ be o - kay._____ 3. The

Verse 3:

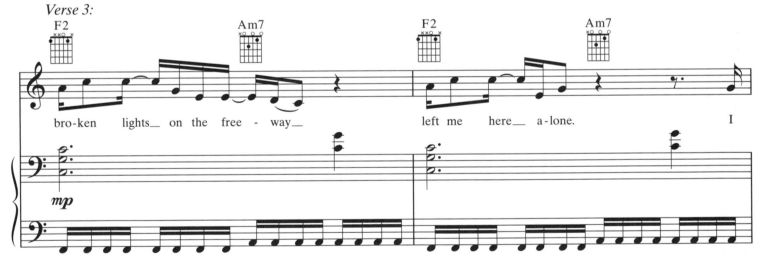

bro-ken lights___ on the free - way___ left me here___ a-lone. I

D.S. 𝄋 al Coda

may have lost___ my way___ now,___ have-n't for-got-ten my way home.___ I'm fall-ing a - part,___

Broken - 8 - 7

CARELESS WHISPER

Words and Music by
GEORGE MICHAEL
and ANDREW RIDGELEY

Moderately ♩ = 76

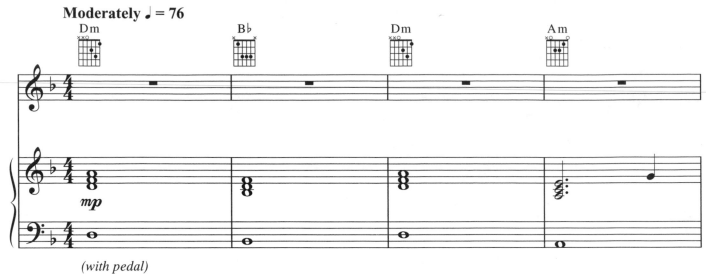

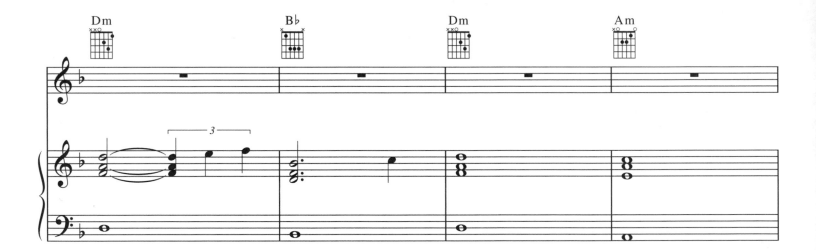

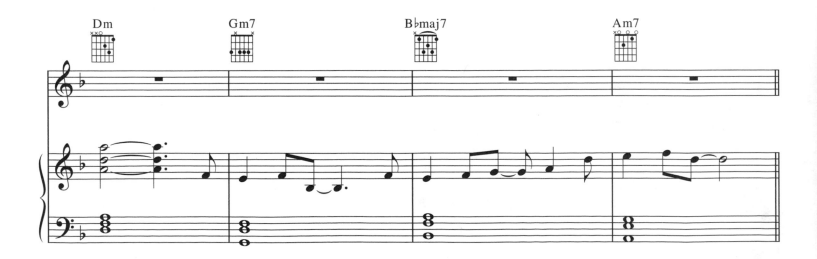

Careless Whisper - 8 - 1

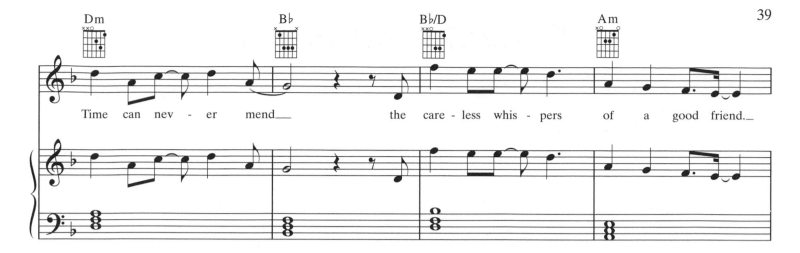

Time can nev - er mend___ the care - less whis - pers of a good friend.___

To the heart and mind___ ig - no-rance is kind.____ But there's no com-fort in the truth,___

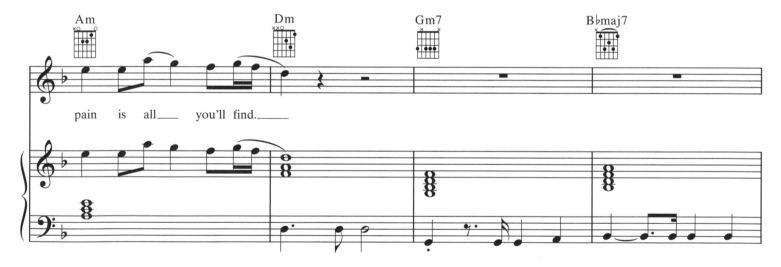

pain is all___ you'll find._____

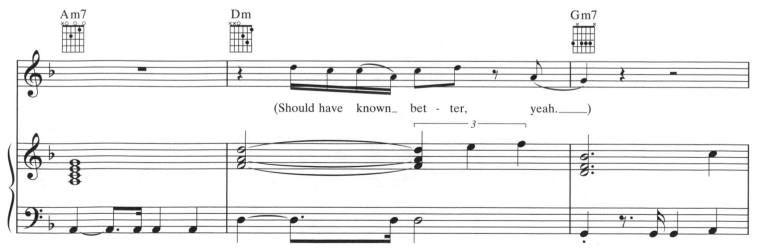

(Should have known_ bet - ter, yeah.___)

Careless Whisper - 8 - 2

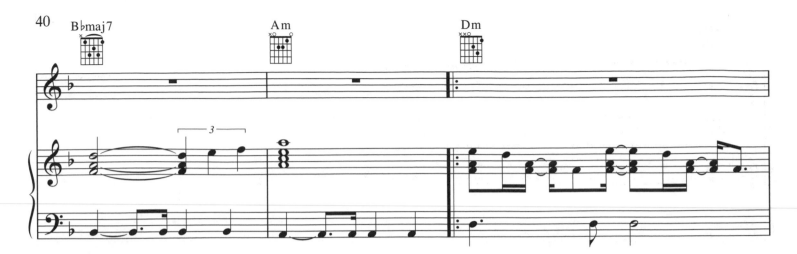

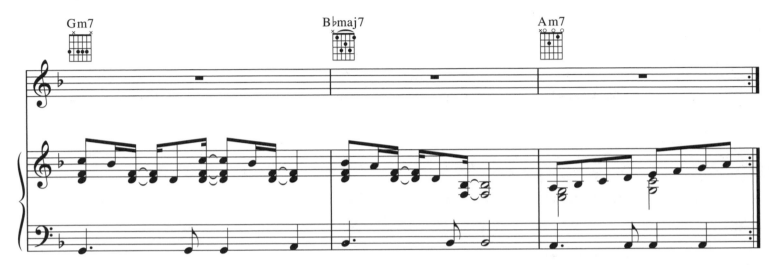

Verse:

1. I feel so___ un - sure___ as I take your hand___ and lead you
2. Time can nev - er mend___ the care - less whis - pers

to the dance floor. As the mu - sic dies,___ some-thing in you eyes___
of a good friend. To the heart and mind___ ig - no - rance is kind.___

calls to mind a sil-ver screen and you're its sad good-bye.
There's no com-fort in the truth, pain is all you'll find.

Chorus:

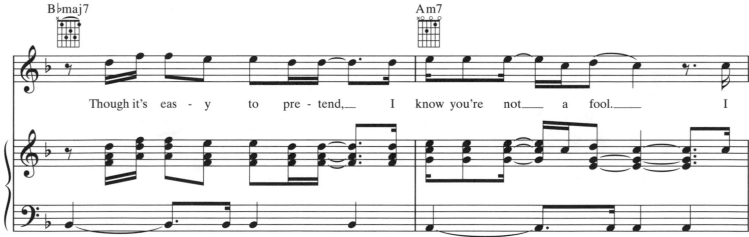

I'm nev-er gon-na dance a-gain, guilt-y feet have got no rhy-thm.

Though it's eas-y to pre-tend, I know you're not a fool. I

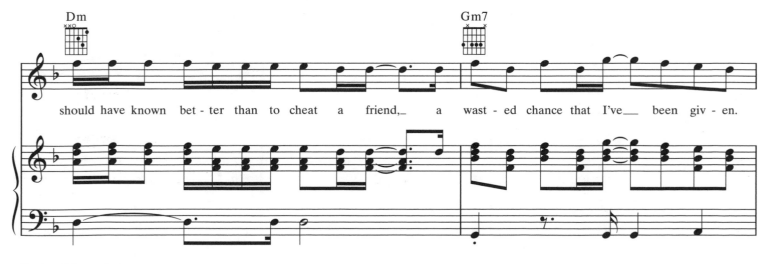

should have known bet-ter than to cheat a friend, a wast-ed chance that I've been giv-en.

42

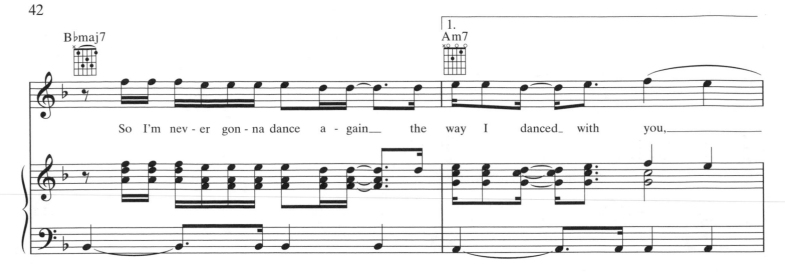

So I'm nev-er gon-na dance a-gain__ the way I danced__ with you,_____

oh,__ oh._____

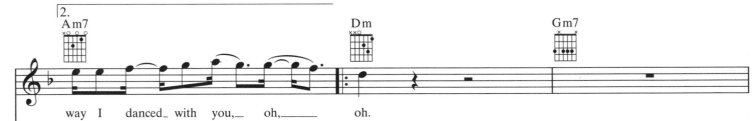

way I danced__ with you,__ oh,_____ oh.

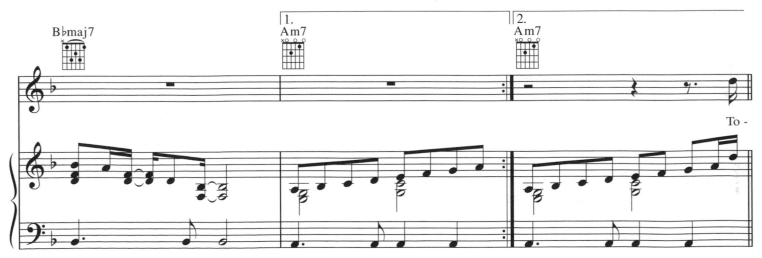

To -

Careless Whisper - 8 - 5

Bridge:

night the mu - sic seems_ so loud.__ I wish that we__ could lose__ this crowd.

May - be it's bet - ter this way, we'd hurt each oth - er with the things we'd want to say.__ We

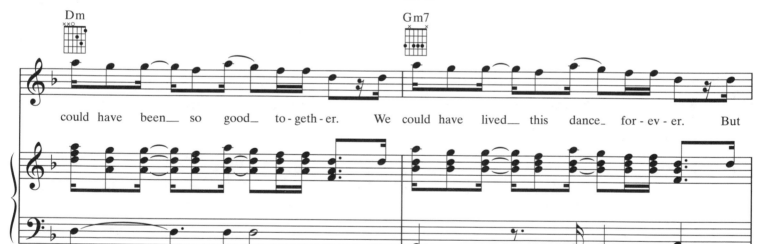

could have been__ so good_ to - geth - er. We could have lived__ this dance_ for - ev - er. But

no_____ one's gon - na dance_ with me,_____ please_ stay._____

Chorus:

CRUSH

Words and Music by
EMANUEL KIRIAKOU,
DAVID HODGES and JESS CATES

48

Crush - 8 - 3

52

Crush - 8 - 7

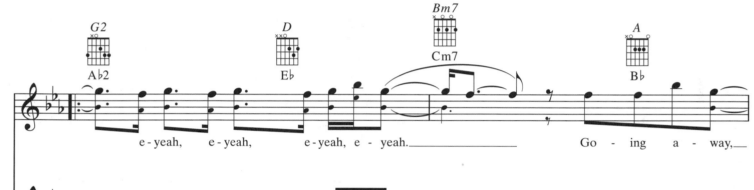

Repeat ad lib. and fade

Crush - 8 - 8

DECODE

Words and Music by
HAYLEY WILLIAMS, JOSH FARRO
and TAYLOR YORK

Moderately slow ♩ = 84

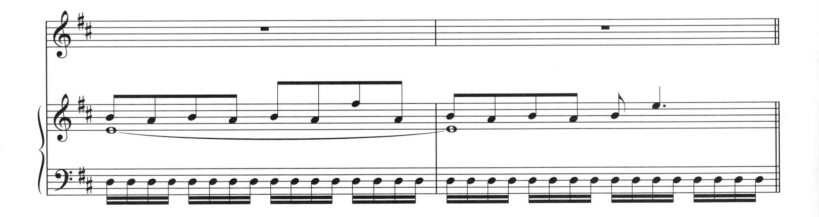

Verse:

1. How can I de-cide____ what's____ right____ when you're cloud-ing up____ my mind?____
2. The truth is hid-ing in____ your____ eyes____ and it's hang-ing on____ your tongue.____

*Original key in B♭m with guitars tuned down a half step.

Decode - 8 - 1

I can't win your los - ing fight___ all the time.
Just boil - ing in my blood,___ but you think that I___ can't

Nor can I ev - er own___ what's___ mine___ when you're al - ways tak - ing sides.___
see what kind of man that___ you___ are, if you're a man___ at all.___

But you won't take a - way___ my pride,___ no, not this___ time.___
Well, I will fig - ure this___ one out___ on my___ own.___

Not this___ time.
On my___ own.
2nd time: (I'm scream - ing I love you so.

Decode - 8 - 2

56

My thoughts you can't de - code.)

cresc.

Chorus:

How did we get here when I used to know you so

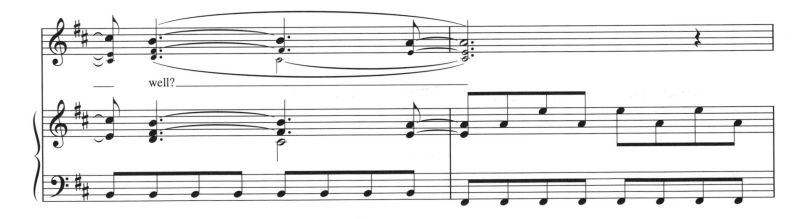

well?

But how did we get here? Well, I think I know.

Decode - 8 - 4

Do you see___

Bridge:

what we've done?___ We've gone and made such

fools of our - selves.___ Do you see___

what we've done?_____ We've gone and made such

fools of our - selves.

Whoa._____

Chorus:

How did we get here when I used to know___ you___ so_____

Decode - 8 - 6

well?_____ Yeah,_____ yeah._____

But how did we get__ here when I used to know__ you__ so_____

_____ well?_____ I think__ I know.__

I think__ I know.__

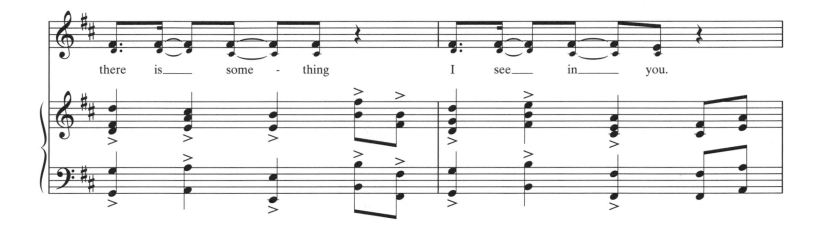

Ooh, there is_____ some - thing I see_____ in_____ you.

It might__ kill_____ me. I want it to____ be true._____

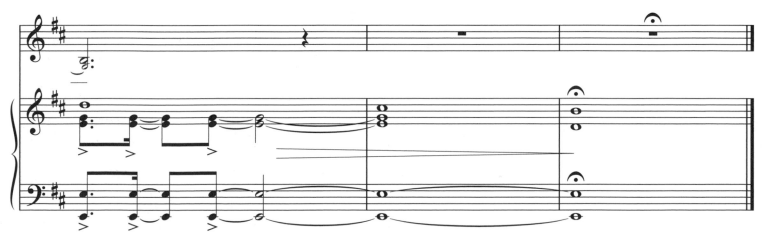

FOOTPRINTS IN THE SAND

Words and Music by
DAVID KREUGER, RICHARD PAGE,
PER OLOF MAGNUSSON and SIMON COWELL

Slowly ♩ = 60

(with pedal)

𝄋 *Verse:*

1. You walked with me,____ foot-prints in the sand,____ and
2. I see my life____ flash a-cross the sky;____ so

helped me un - der - stand____ where I'm go - in'.
man - y times____ have I____ been so a - fraid.____

64

spair.___ I'll car-ry you   when you need a   friend.___   You'll find_

___ my foot-prints in___ the sand.

Bridge:

When I'm wea-ry,   well, I know you'll be there,_ and I_____ can feel you

when you_____ say..._____   I prom-ise

Footprints in the Sand - 4 - 3

Chorus:

15 STEP

Words and Music by THOMAS YORKE,
JONATHAN GREENWOOD, COLIN GREENWOOD,
EDWARD O'BRIEN and PHILIP SELWAY

15 Steps - 7 - 1

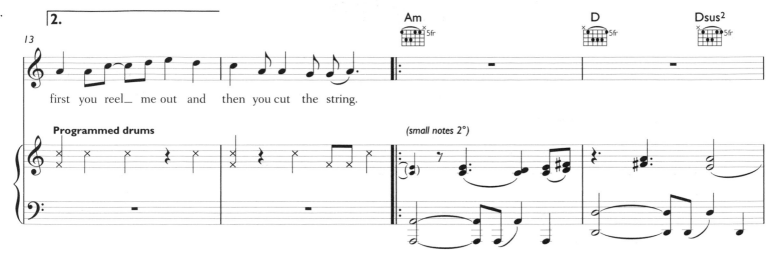

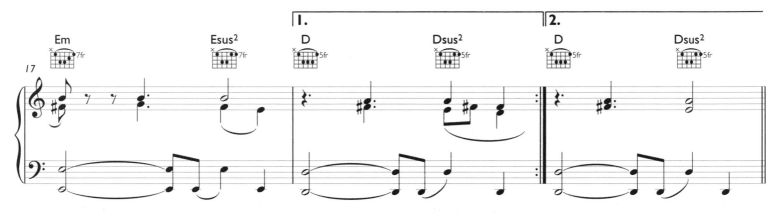

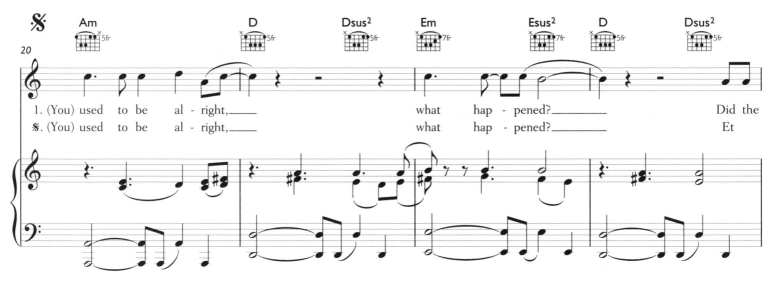

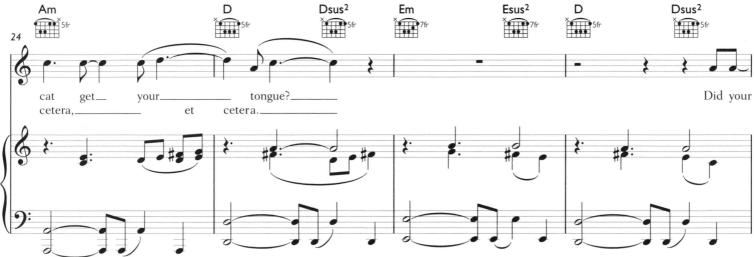

68

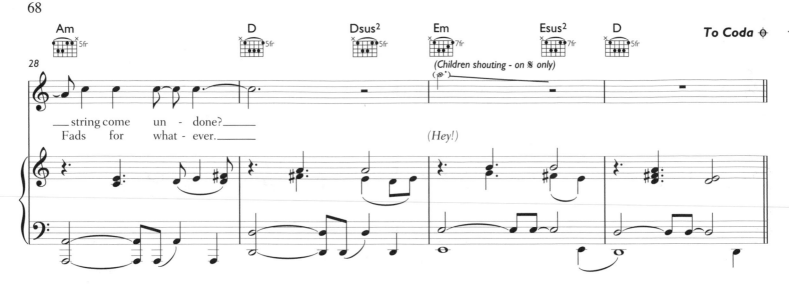

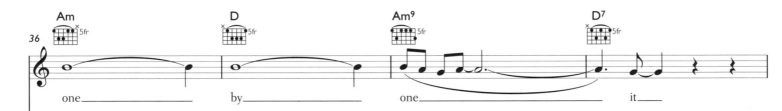

15 Steps - 7 - 3

soft _____ as your _____ pil - low. _____

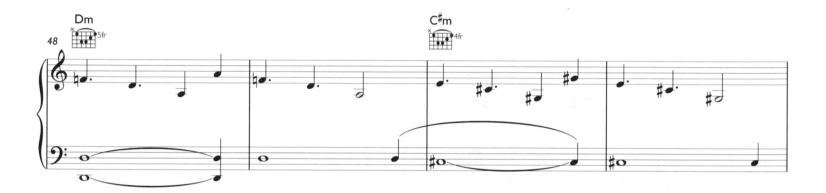

D.𝄋 al Coda

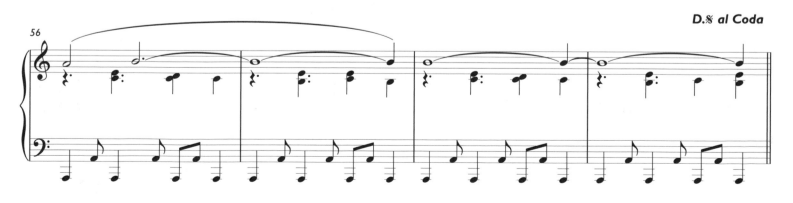

70

72

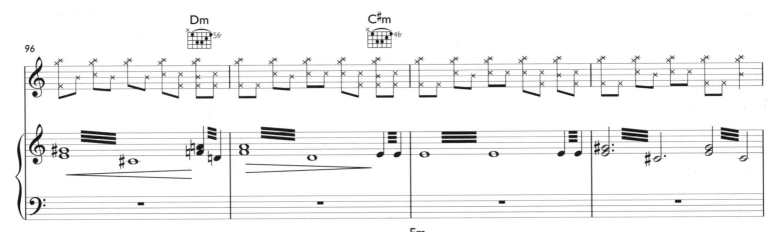

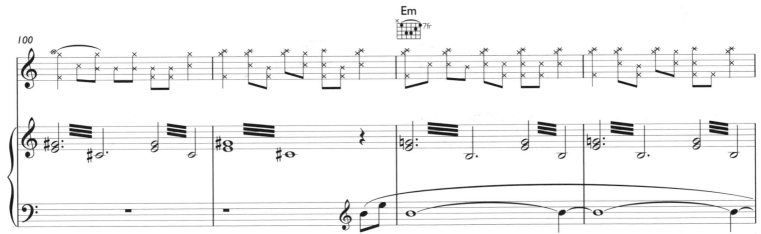

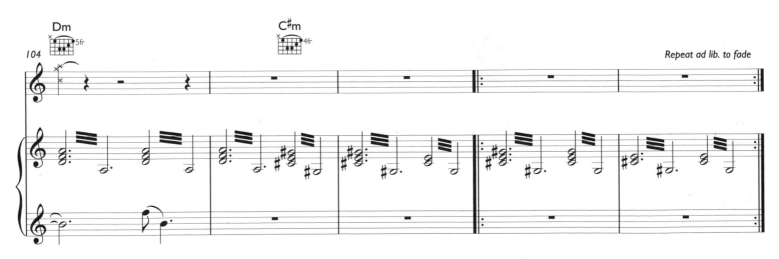

15 Steps - 7 - 7

HOME SWEET HOME

Words and Music by
NIKKI SIXX, VINCE NEIL
and TOMMY LEE

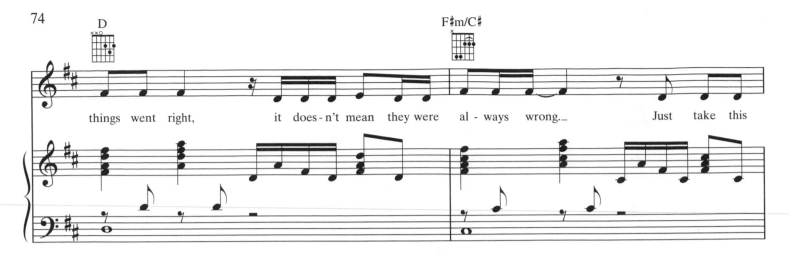

things went right, it does-n't mean they were al-ways wrong.__ Just take this

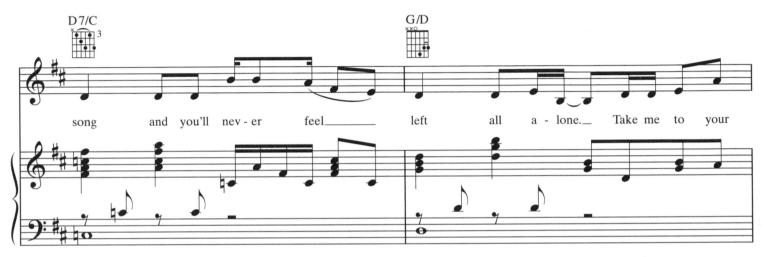

song and you'll nev-er feel_____ left all a-lone.__ Take me to your

heart, feel me in your bones. Just one more

night, and I'm com-ing off__ this long and wind-ing road.__ I'm on my

Chorus:

way,_____ I'm on my way_____ home, sweet,___

home._____ To - night, to - night,___ I'm on my

way,_____ I'm on my way_____ home, sweet,___

home._____ 2. You know__ that I've

Chorus:

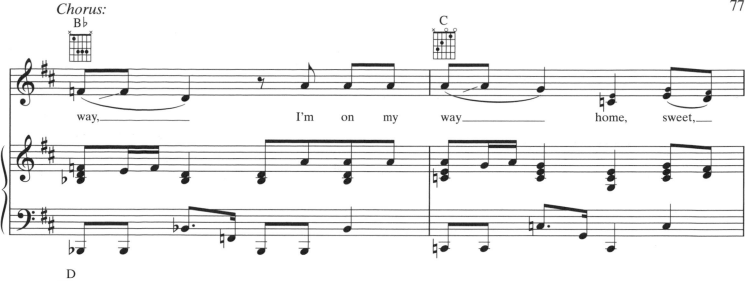

way,_____ I'm on my way_____ home, sweet,____

home._____ To - night, to - night,___ I'm on my

way,_____ just set me free,___ home, sweet,____

home._____
(Inst. solo ad lib....

78

GOTTA BE SOMEBODY

Lyrics by
CHAD KROEGER

Music by
NICKELBACK

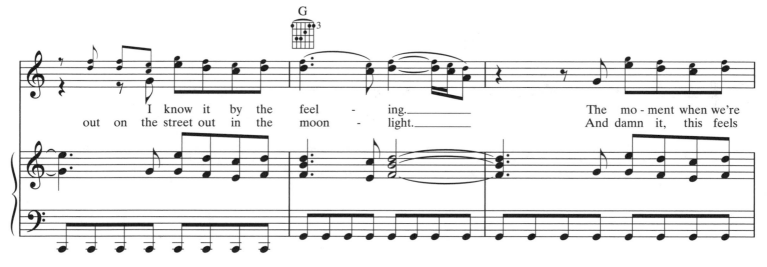

got-ta be some-bod-y for me like that. 'Cause no-bod-y wants___ to go it

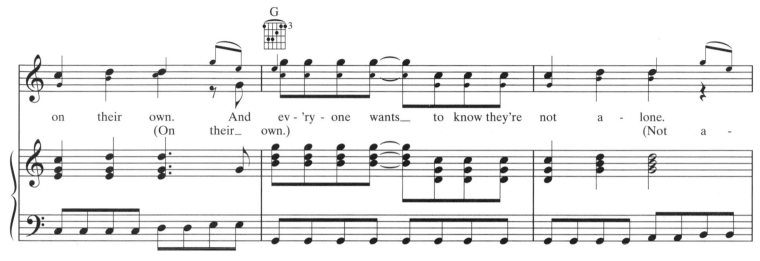

on their own. And ev-'ry-one wants___ to know they're not a - lone.
(On their___ own.) (Not a -

Some-bod-y else___ that feels the same some - where. There's got-ta be some-bod-y for
lone.) (Same some - where.)

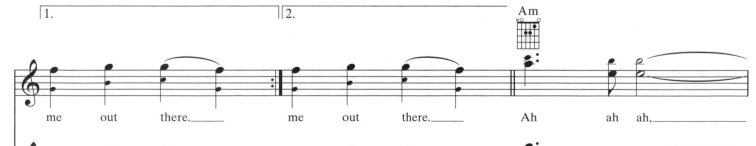

1.   2.   Am

me out there.___   me out there.___   Ah   ah   ah,_____

on their own. And ev-'ry-one wants___ to know they're not a - lone.
(On their___ own.) (Not a -

Some-bod - y else___ that feels the same some - where. There's got - ta be some - bod - y for
lone.) (Same some - where.)

me out there.___ No - bod - y wants___ to be the last one there. 'Cause

(When you're look - in' for...)

ev - 'ry - one wants_ to feel like some - one cares. Some-bod - y else__ that feels the

(When there's_ no...__)

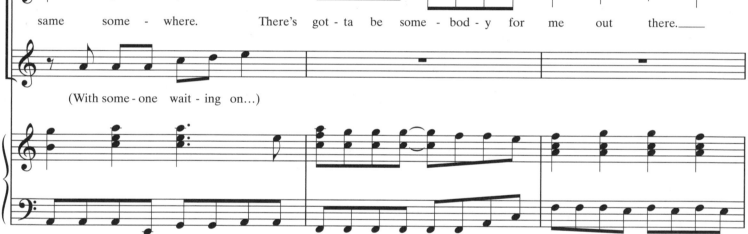

same some - where. There's got - ta be some - bod - y for me out there.___

(With some - one wait - ing on...)

decresc.

rit.

HOT N' COLD

Words and Music by
KATY PERRY, LUKASZ GOTTWALD
and MAX MARTIN

Moderately fast ♩ = 132

Verse:

1. You change your mind____ like a girl____ chang-es clothes.____
2. We used to be____ just like twins,____ so in sync.____

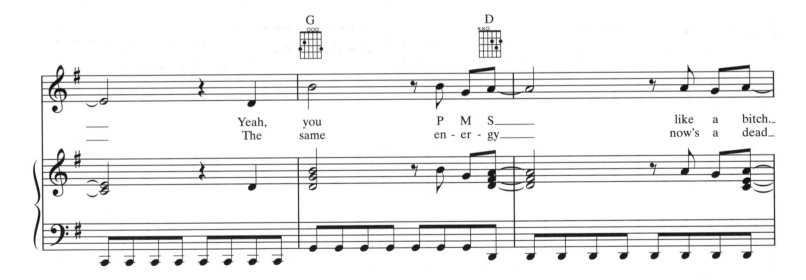

Yeah, you P M S____ like a bitch.____
The you same en-er-gy____ now's a dead____

I would know.____ And you o-ver-think,
bat-ter-y.____ Used to laugh 'bout noth-ing.____

Hot n' Cold - 6 - 1

92

Hot n' Cold - 6 - 5

93

Hot n' Cold - 6 - 6

I HATE THIS PART

Words and Music by
MICH HANSEN, JONAS JEBERG,
LUCAS SECON and WAYNE HECTOR

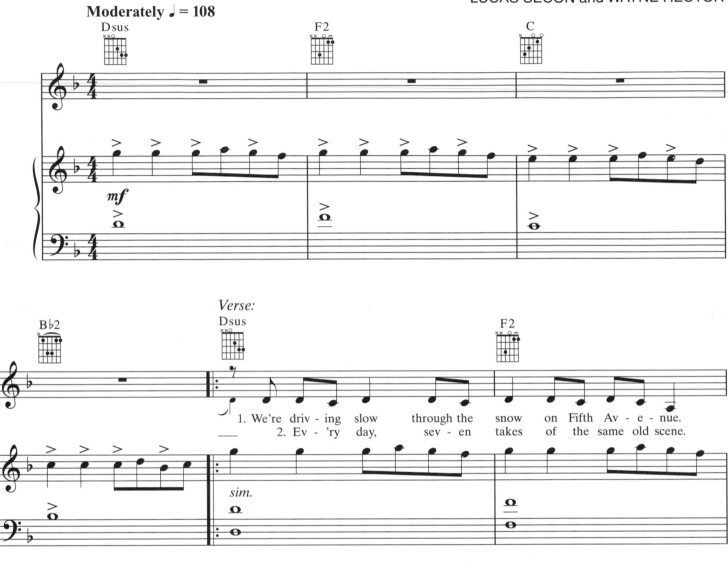

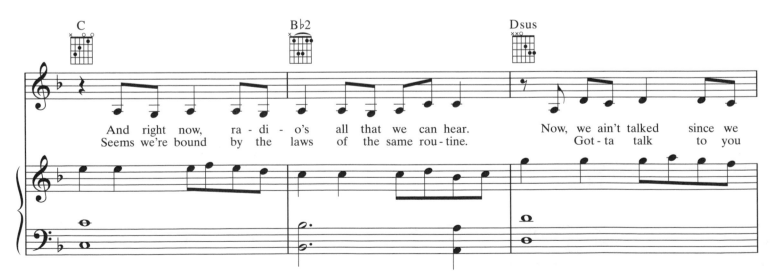

96

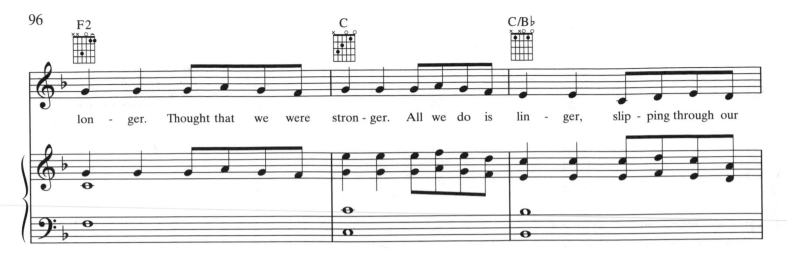

lon - ger. Thought that we were stron - ger. All we do is lin - ger, slip - ping through our

fin - gers. I don't wan - na try now. All that's left's good - bye, to find a way that

I can tell you._____ I hate this part right here.

I hate this part right here. I just can't

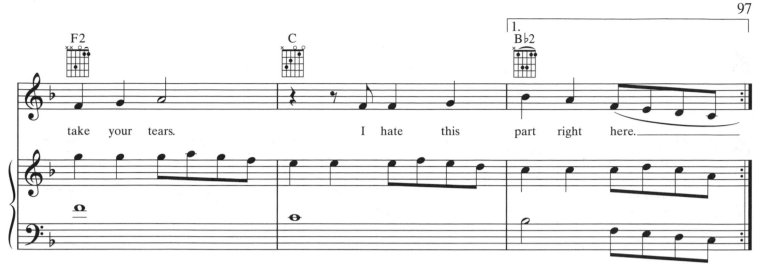

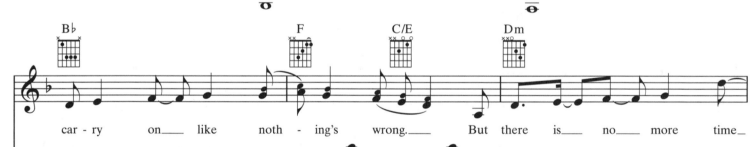

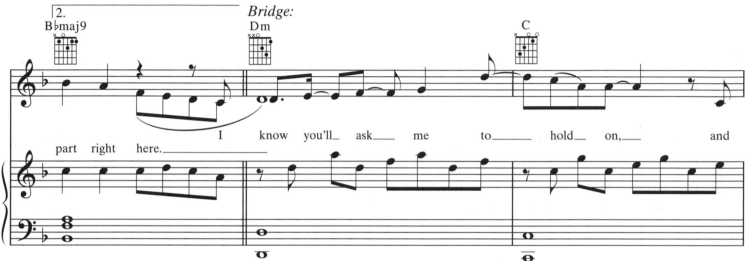

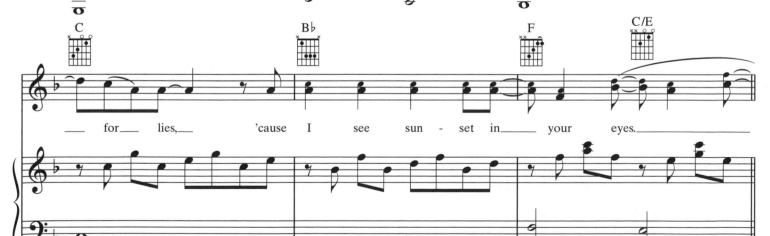

I Hate This Part - 6 - 4

Chorus:

I can't take it an-y lon - ger. Thought that we were stron - ger. All we do is lin - ger, slip-ping through our fin - gers. I don't wan-na try now. All that's left's good - bye, to find a way that I can tell you_____ that I got-ta do it,_____ I got-ta do it,_____ I got-ta do it._____ I hate_ this_

IF TODAY WAS YOUR LAST DAY

Words and Music by
CHAD KROEGER

102 *Chorus:*

If Today Was Your Last Day - 9 - 3

104

If Today Was Your Last Day - 9 - 5

107

If Today Was Your Last Day - 9 - 8

108

LET IT ROCK

Words and Music by
KEVIN RUDOLF and DWAYNE CARTER

Let It Rock - 7 - 1

112

Let It Rock - 7 - 4

LIVE YOUR LIFE

Words and Music by
CLIFFORD HARRIS, MAKEBA RIDDICK,
JUSTIN SMITH and MIHAI BALAN DAN

Moderately slow ♩ = 84

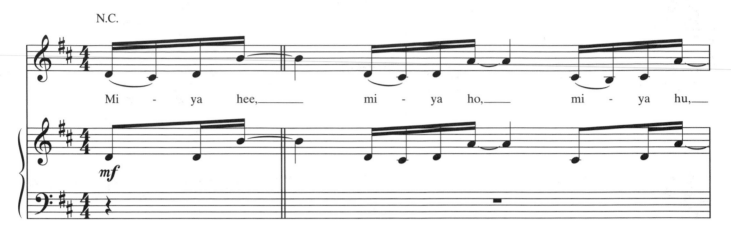

118

You stead-y chas-in' that pa - per. Just live your life,_____ ay._____

Ain't got no time for no hat - ers. Just live your life,_____ ay.

No tell-in' where it will take_____ ya. Just live your life,_____ ay._____

'Cause I'm a pa - per chas - er, just liv-in' my life,_____ my life,_____ my life,_____

my life.___ Just liv - in' my life,___ my life,___ my life,___

my life.___ Just liv - in' my life.___

Verse:
N.C.

1. *Never mind what haters say, ignore them 'til they fade away.*
2. *See additional lyrics*

Amazing they ungrateful after all the game I gave away. *Safe to say I paved the way for you cats to get paid today.*

You'd still be wasting days away now had I never saved the day. *Consider them my protégé, homage I think they should pay.*

120

Instead of being gracious, they violate in a major way.   *I never been a hater, still I love them in a crazy way.*

G   D

Some say they sold the yay and know they couldn't get work on Labor Day. It ain't that black and white, it has an area the shade of gray.

A   Bm   G   D

I'm Westside anyway, even if I left today and stayed away.   *Some move away to make a way, not move away 'cause they afraid.*

A   Bm   G   D

I brought back to the hood and all you ever did was take away. I pray for patience, but they make me wanna melt their face away.

122

123

Live Your Life - 9 - 8

mi - ya ha___ ha. Mi - ya hee,___ ___ mi - ya ha___ ha. So live your life.___

Verse 2:
I'm the opposite of moderate, immaculately polished with
The spirit of a hustler and the swagger of a college kid.
Allergic to the counterfeit, impartial to the politics,
*Articulate, but still I'll grab a n***** by the collar quick.*

Whoever having problems with their record sales just holla till.
If that don't work and all else fails, then turn around and follow till.
I got love for the game but, ay, I'm not in love with all of it.
'Could do without the fame and the rappers nowadays are comedy.

The hootin' and the hollerin', back and forth with the arguing,
Where you from, who you know, what you make, and what kind of car you in.
Seems as though you lost sight of what's important when depositin'
Them checks into your bank account and you up out of poverty.

Your values is a disarray, prioritizing horribly,
Unhappy with your riches 'cause you're piss-poor morally,
Ignoring all prior advice and forewarning.
And we mighty full of ourselves all of a sudden, aren't we?
(To Chorus:)

MY LIFE WOULD SUCK WITHOUT YOU

Words and Music by
CLAUDE KELLY, LUKASZ GOTTWALD
and MAX MARTIN

My Life Would Suck Without You - 7 - 1

126

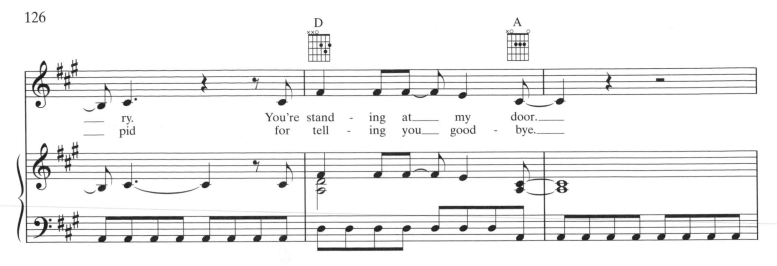

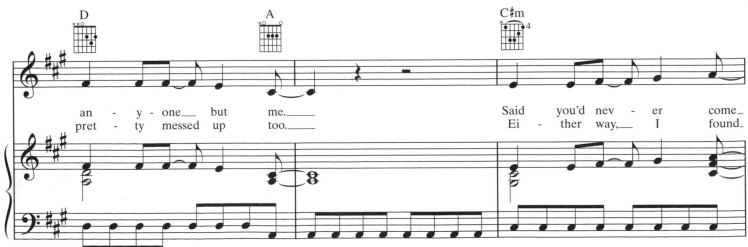

My Life Would Suck Without You - 7 - 2

I real-ly should-n't miss_____ you,_____ but

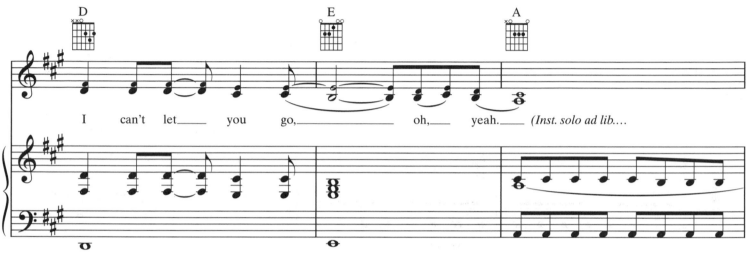

I can't let_____ you go,_____ oh,___ yeah._____ *(Inst. solo ad lib....*

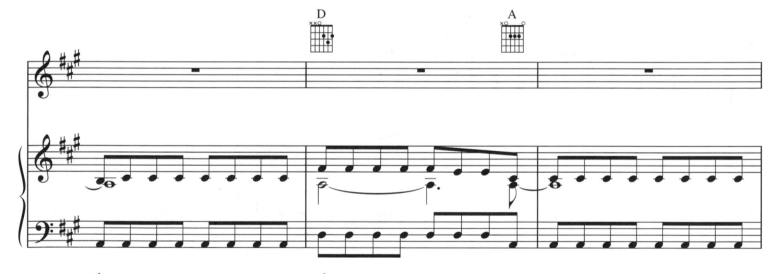

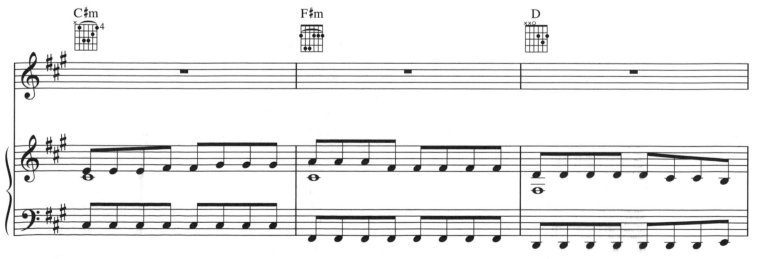

My Life Would Suck Without You - 7 - 7

NEVER FAR AWAY

Words and Music by
WES WILLIS, KEVIN HUGULEY
and JASON INGRAM

Slowly ♩ = 80

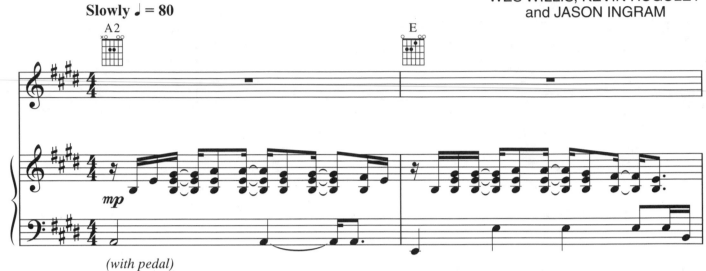

(with pedal)

Verses 1 & 2:

1. An-oth-er mile_____ down_ the road,_____
2. I close my eyes_____ and try_____ to see,_____

134

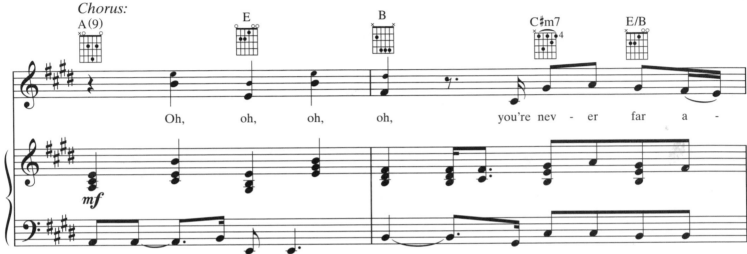

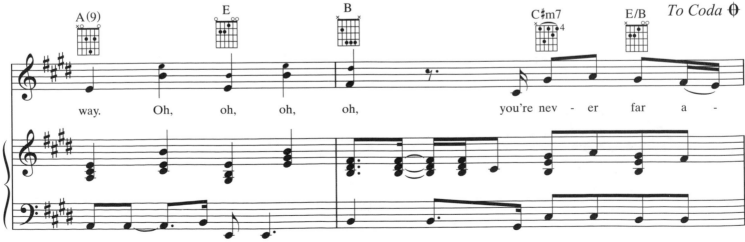

ONE STEP AT A TIME

Words and Music by
MICH HANSEN, JONAS JEBERG,
ROBBIE NEVIL and LAUREN EVANS

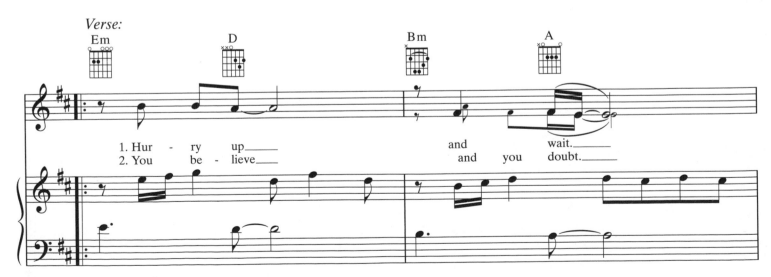

*Original recording in D♭ major.

One Step At a Time - 6 - 1

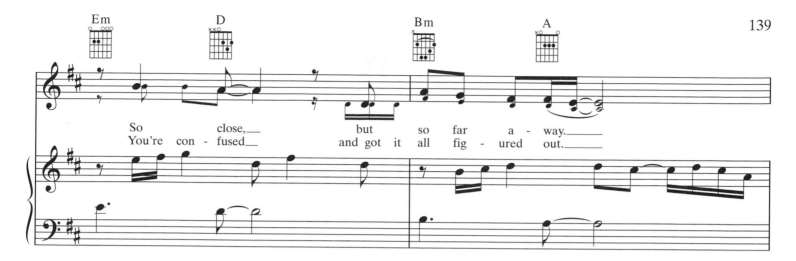

So close,___ but so far a-way.___
You're con-fused___ and got it all fig-ured out.___

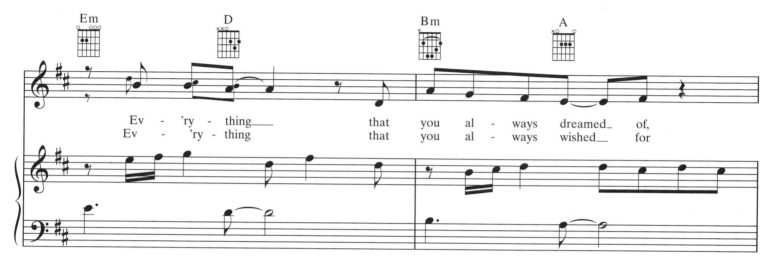

Ev-'ry-thing___ that you al-ways dreamed_ of,
Ev-'ry-thing that you al-ways wished_ for

close e-nough for you to taste, but you just___ can't touch.___
could be yours, should be yours, would be yours if they on-ly knew.___

You wan-na show the world, but no one knows your name yet.

One Step At a Time - 6 - 2

Chorus:

step at a time.___ There's no need to rush.__ It's like learn-ing to fly___ or

fall-ing in love.___ It's gon-na hap-pen and it's sup-posed to hap-pen that we

find the rea - sons why,___ one step at a time.___ Da da da da da da

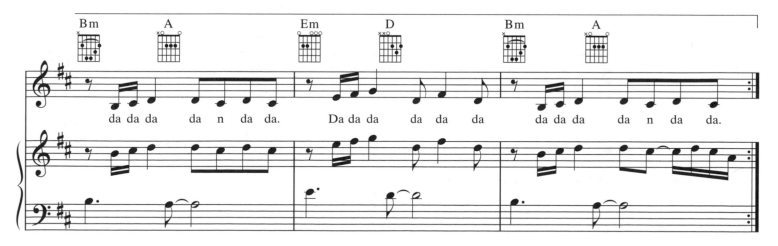

da da da da n da da. Da da da da da da da da da da n da da.

142

One Step At a Time - 6 - 5

143

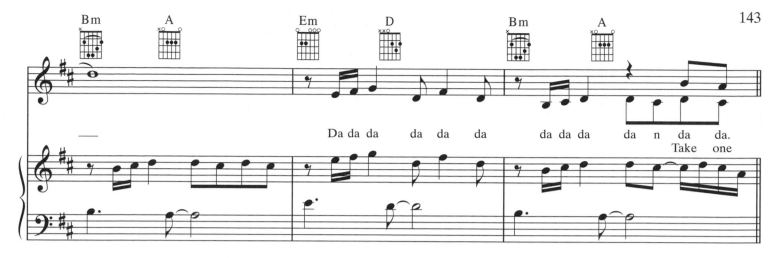

Chorus:

One Step At a Time - 6 - 6

SECOND CHANCE

Words and Music by
DAVE BASSETT and BRENT SMITH

SHUTTIN' DETROIT DOWN

Words and Music by
JOHN RICH and
JOHN D. ANDERSON

150

*Play G 2nd time.

while the boss____ man takes his bo - nus pay____ and jets____

____ on out____ of town.____ And D. C.'s bail - ing out____ them bank-

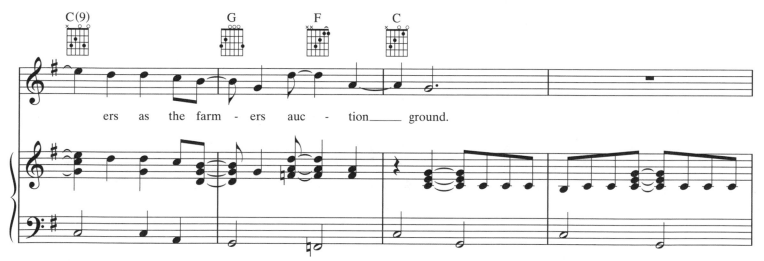

ers as the farm - ers auc - tion____ ground.

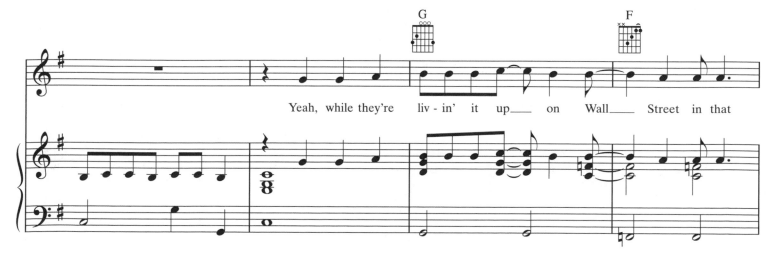

Yeah, while they're liv - in' it up____ on Wall____ Street in that

152

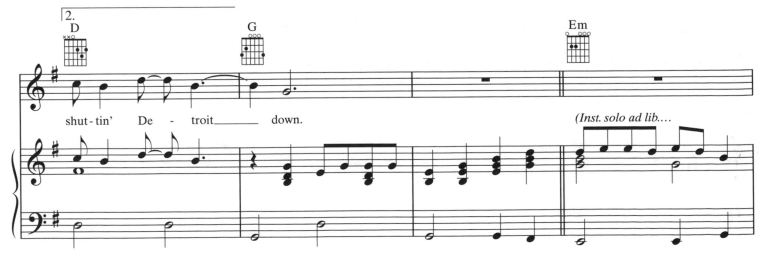

Shuttin' Detroit Down - 7 - 5

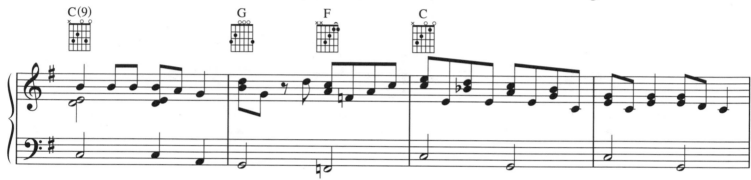

...end solo) Yeah, while they're liv-in' it up___ on Wall_

__ Street in that New York Cit-y town, here in the real___ world,_ they're

154

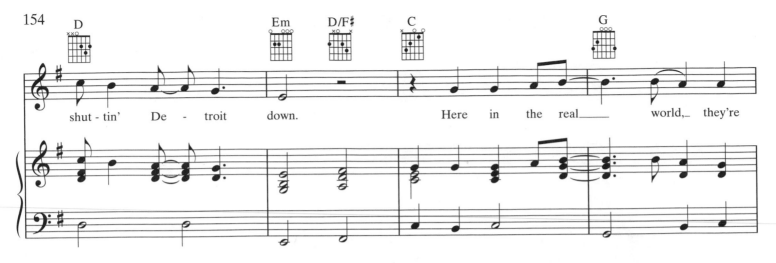

shut-tin' De - troit down. Here in the real___ world,___ they're

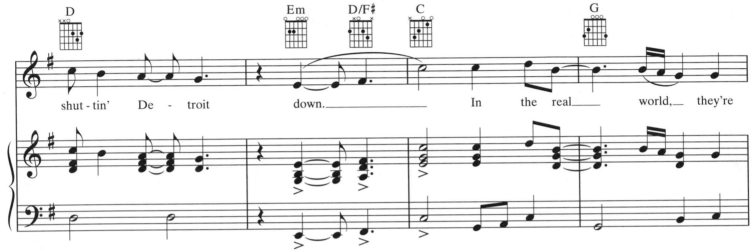

shut-tin' De - troit down._____ In the real___ world,___ they're

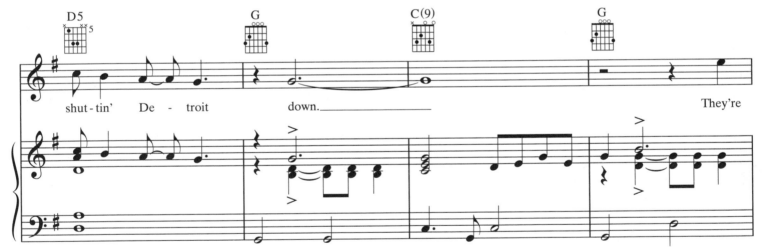

shut-tin' De - troit down._____ They're

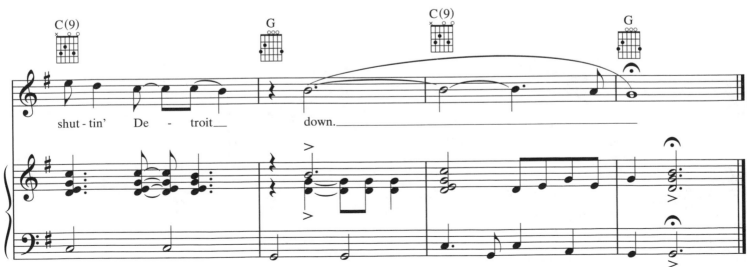

shut-tin' De - troit___ down._____

STUCK WITH EACH OTHER

Words and Music by
DIANE WARREN

Moderately slow ♩ = 84

Verse:

1. You can___ think you can get___ free, think you won't need___ me,
2. I can___ say I would not___ care if you were not___ there,

that you're gon - na get you some - thin' bet - ter, but you know that you're in this for - ev - er.
tell my - self that I'd do fine with - out you, but I'd die if I was not a - round you.

You can___ think you can walk___ out, e - ven have your___ doubts,
I can___ try to con - vince___ you I don't need to be with___ you,

Stuck With Each Other - 5 - 1

Chorus:

SUPERMASSIVE BLACK HOLE

Words and Music by
MATTHEW JAMES BELLAMY

Moderately ♩ = 126

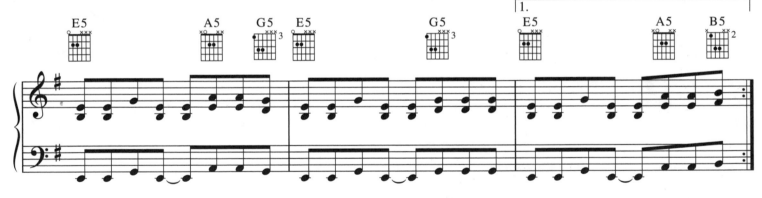

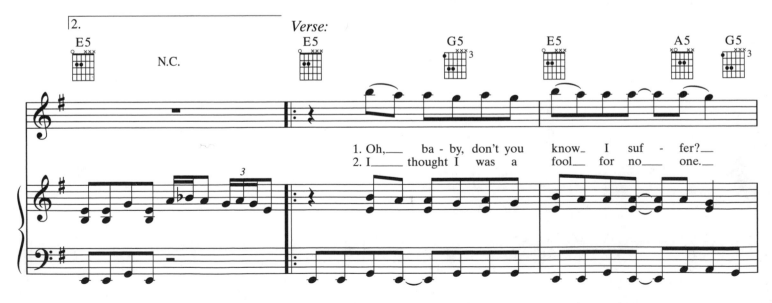

1. Oh,___ ba - by, don't you know___ I suf - fer?___
2. I___ thought I was a fool___ for no___ one.___

Supermassive Black Hole - 5 - 1

162

THINKING OF YOU

Words and Music by
KATY PERRY

166

I guess sec-ond best_ is all I___ will_____ know. 'Cause when

he pulled me in, I was dis - gust-ed with_ my - self.____ 'Cause when

Chorus:

I'm with him, I am think-ing of you,___ think-ing of you.___

What you would do_____ if you were the one who was spend-ing the night?_

my-self let you go.

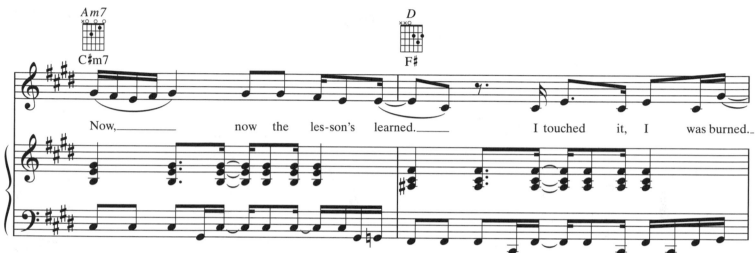

Now, now the les-son's learned. I touched it, I was burned.

Oh, I think you should know. 'Cause when

Chorus:

I'm with him, I am think-ing of you,

Thinking of You - 7 - 5

170

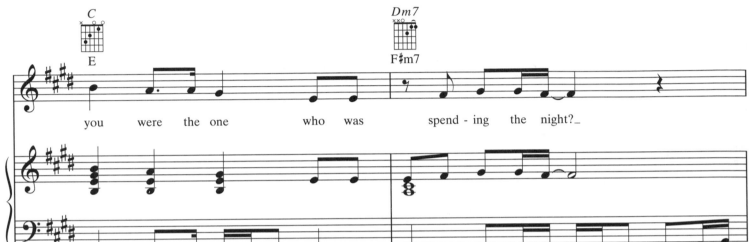

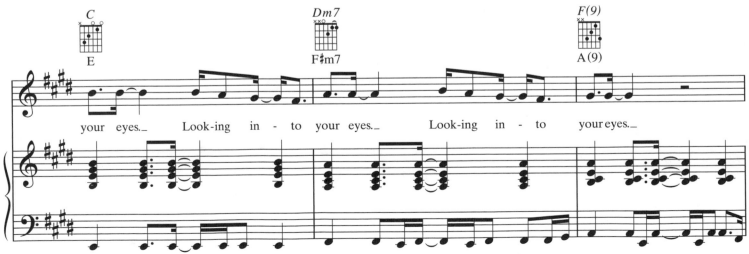

Thinking of You - 7 - 6

WHAT ABOUT NOW

Words and Music by
BEN MOODY, DAVID HODGES
and JOSH HARTZLER

Verses 2 & 3:

2. Change the col - ors of___ the sky___ and o - pen up___ to_____
3. The sun is break - ing in___ your eyes___ to start a new___ day.___

the ways you made___ me feel___ a - live,___ the ways I loved___ you.
This bro - ken heart___ can still___ sur - vive___ with a touch of your___ grace.

For all the things___ that nev - er died___ to make it through___ the night._
As shad - ows fade___ in - to___ the light,___ I am by___ your side_

___ Love___ will find___ you.} What a - bout___ now?___
___ where love___ will find___ you.}

What About Now - 6 - 2

174

What About Now - 6 - 3

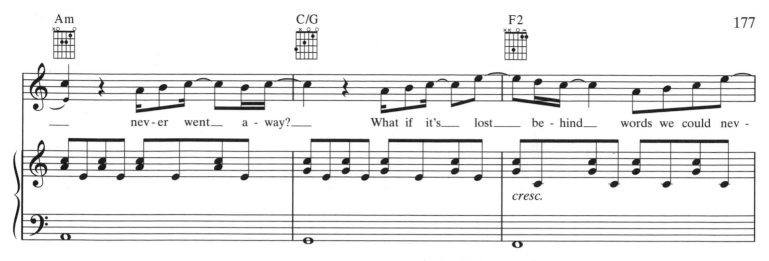

nev-er went_ a-way?__ What if it's_ lost_ be-hind_ words we could nev-

cresc.

D.S. %̸ al Coda

er find?_ What a-bout_ now?_

⊕ *Coda*

____ Ba-by, be-fore____

it's_ too_ late,__ ba-by, be-fore____ it's_ too_ late,_

_____ what a-bout_ now?_____

WHAT DO I DO WITH MY HEART

Words and Music by
GLENN FREY and DON HENLEY

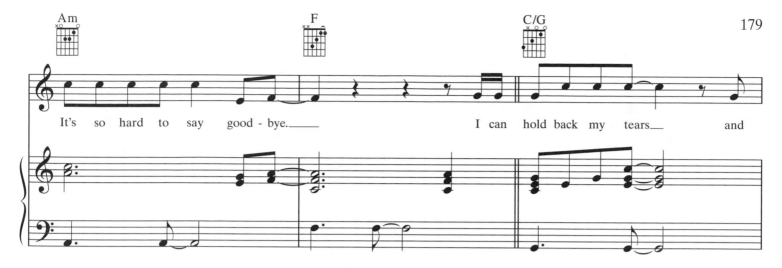

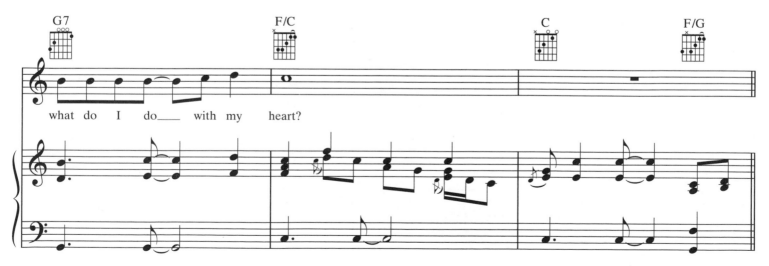

180

183

What Do I Do with My Heart - 6 - 6

WHATEVER YOU LIKE

Words and Music by
CLIFFORD HARRIS, DAVID SIEGEL
and JAMES SCHEFFER

Whatever You Like - 7 - 1

186

Whatever You Like - 7 - 3

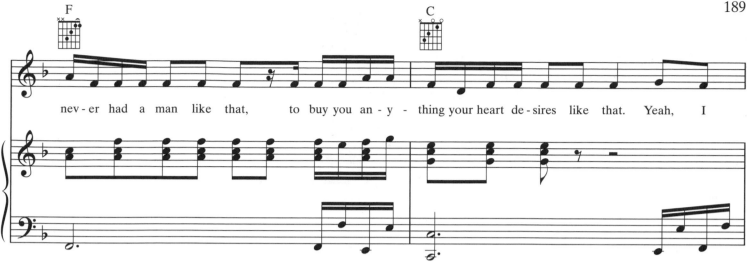

never had a man like that, to buy you an-y-thing your heart de-sires like that. Yeah, I

want your bod-y, need your bod-y. Long as you got me, you won't need no-bod-y. You

D.S. % al Coda

want it, I got it, go get it, I'll buy it. Tell them oth-er broke n**-**** be qui-et. Stacks on

Whatever You Like - 7 - 6

Repeat ad lib. and fade

WHAT'S RIGHT IS RIGHT

Words and Music by
DENNIS MORGAN and SIMON CLIMIE

Moderately slow ♩ = 84

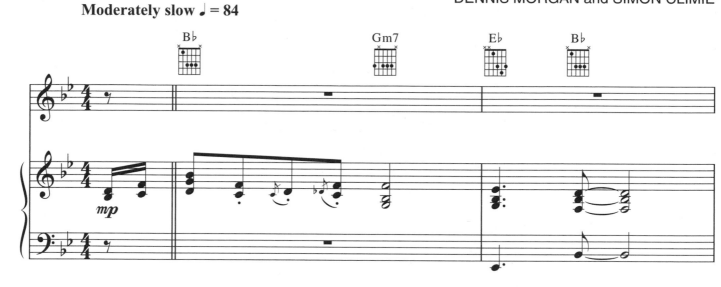

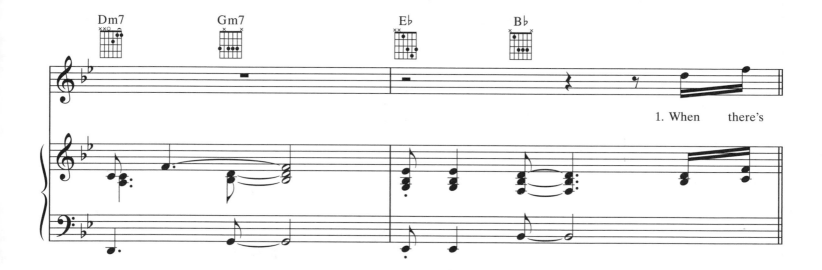

1. When there's

Verse 1:

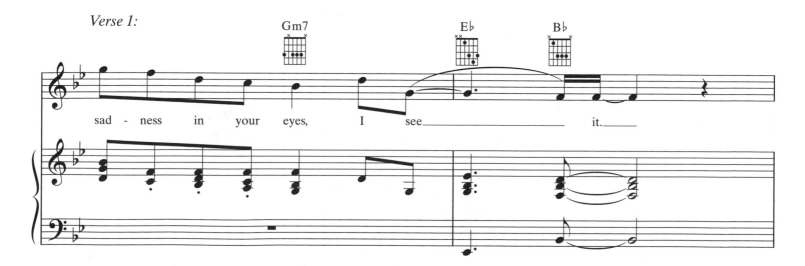

sad - ness in your eyes, I see _____ it. _____

What's Right Is Right - 7 - 1

194

Verses 3 & 4:

3. This I prom - ise you for - ev - er._____ I'm
4. *(Inst. solo ad lib....*

with you all the___ way to the fin - ish line._____ And

we're gon - na cross that bridge to - geth - er,_____ march - ing

step by step,___ walk - ing side by side. *...end solo)* I don't wan - na go_____

𝄋 *Chorus:*

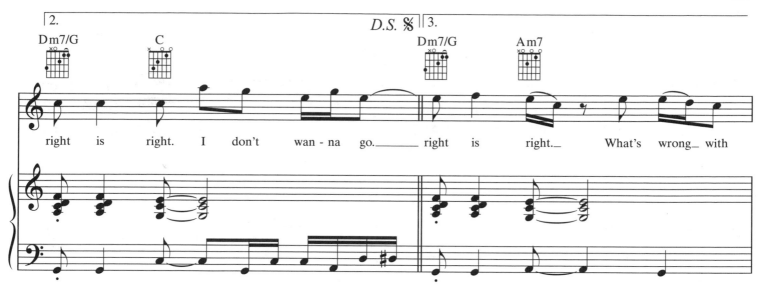

What's Right Is Right - 7 - 7

YOU PULLED ME THROUGH

Words and Music by
DIANE WARREN

WORKING ON A DREAM

Words and Music by
BRUCE SPRINGSTEEN

Moderately ♩ = 112

1. Out here, the nights are long,___ the

days are lone - ly. I think of you___ and I'm work-ing on a dream.___

___ I'm work-ing on a dream.___

Verses 2, 3, & 4:

2. Now the cards I've drawn,___ it's a rough hand, dar - lin'. I
3. Rain pour-ing down,___ I swing my ham-mer. My
4. *(Whistling...*

straight-en my back___ and I'm work-ing on a dream.___
hands are rough___ from work-ing on a dream.___

204

Chorus:

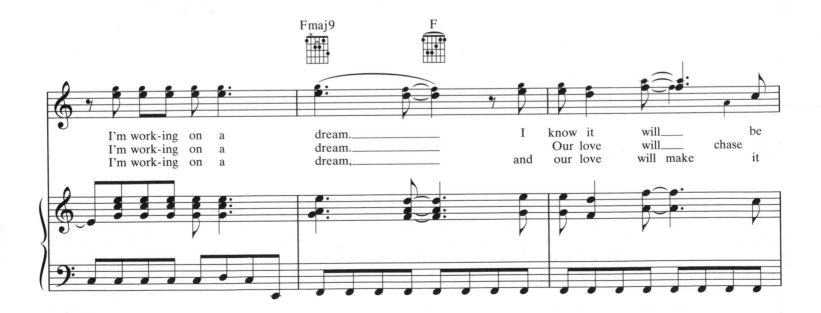

mine some-day.___
trou-ble a-way.___
real some-day.___

Verse 5:

5. Sun-rise come,___ I climb the lad-der. A new day breaks___ and

I'm work-ing on a dream. I'm work-ing on a

dream.___ I'm work-ing on a dream._____

206